Happy

From

Love. Ally . . .

CW00739901

o's !

First Published in Great Britain by
Powerfresh Limited
3 Gray Street
Northampton
England
NN1 3QQ

Telephone 0604 30996 Country Code 44
Facsimile 0604 21013

NOW WE ARE 40
ISBN 1 874125 14 7

Printed in Britain by Avalon Print Ltd., Northampton.

NOW WE ARE

40

by J.P

HAPPY BIRTHDAY TO YOU,
HAPPY BIRTHDAY TO YOU,
HAPPY BIRTHDAY
FORTY PHOBIA,
HAPPY BIRTHDAY TO YOU!

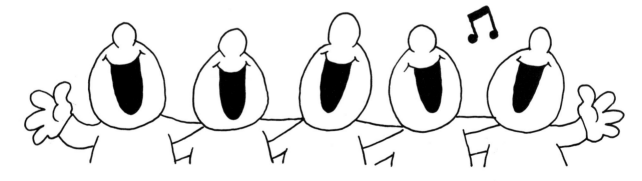

BEING 40 CAN BE A TIME OF DISCOVERY..

ON HIS 40TH BIRTHDAY BOB DISCOVERED THAT HE WAS NO LONGER WORRIED ABOUT BEING 40 YEARS OLD – HE WAS NOW WORRIED ABOUT BEING 40 MILLION LIGHT YEARS FROM BRIGHTON !

ALICE WAS
HORRIFIED TO
DISCOVER THAT
SHE COULDN'T
SEE HER NAVEL
ANYMORE!

BEING 40 HELPED PETER TO DISCOVER THE CHILD WITHIN!

WALLY DISCOVERED
THAT MOLLY HAD
LEFT THE SUPERGLUE
NEXT TO HIS TUBE
OF PILE CREAM!
HE ALSO DISCOVERED
A CURE FOR WIND!

ON HER 40TH BIRTHDAY MARY DISCOVERED THAT EVEN THOUGH SHE COULD STILL GET IN TO A PAIR OF SIZE 10 LEVI'S, SHE WOULD PROBABLY HAVE TO HAVE THEM SURGICALLY REMOVED!

THE 40 PLUS SURVIVAL KIT—FOR HIM!

CHECK THIS LIST TO SEE IF YOU HAVE GOT EVERYTHING YOU NEED!

1. HAIR DYE AND/OR TOUPEE
2. LOW FAT FOODS AND VITAMIN PILLS
3. FITNESS VIDEO (TO WATCH ONLY)
4. NEW SPORTY CAR WITH LOUD STEREO
5. LATEST CHART AND RAVE TAPES
6. YOUNG BLOND BIMBO - 38-24-36
7. SEX GUIDE VIDEO (TO WATCH ONLY)
8. MEMBERSHIP OF NIGHT CLUB (DON'T DANCE!)
9. REGULAR VISITS TO PSYCHOTHERAPIST
10. SYMPATHETIC BANK MANAGER

THE 40 PLUS SURVIVAL KIT — FOR HER!

1 HAIR COLOUR AND VARIOUS WIGS
2 DIET AND SLIMMING MAGAZINES
3 EXERCISE VIDEO (WATCH ONLY)
4 NEW SEXY UNDERWEAR
5 AEROBICS CLUB MEMBERSHIP (DON'T GO)
6 REGULAR MASSAGE AND SUNBED SESSIONS
7 TOYBOY — 6 FT. TALL BODYBUILDER
8 COSMETIC SURGERY AND LIPOSUCTION
9 JOIN A WOMEN'S STUDIES GROUP
10 SECRET SUPPLY OF CHOCOLATES

OK? NOW GO FOR IT!

WHEN THE PARACHUTE CLUB GAVE JONATHAN A SPECIAL BIRTHDAY JUMP
THEY FORGOT TO GIVE HIM A SPECIAL BIRTHDAY PARACHUTE!

SUE HAD CAREFULLY KEPT HER REAL AGE SECRET FROM EVERYONE,
EXCEPT HER IMMEDIATE FAMILY!

GEORGE HAD NOT EXPECTED THE GUYS TO HIRE A STRIPOGRAM GIRL AND NONE OF THEM HAD EXPECTED HER TO GO SO FAR!

TONY'S WORKMATES HAD ONE FINAL BIRTHDAY SURPRISE
FOR HIM—THEY HAD HIRED A CONTRACT KILLER!

WHEN LISA CAME OUT OF THE BATHROOM
SHE FOUND THAT DAVE HAD INVITED ALL THEIR FRIENDS IN FOR
HER SURPRISE BIRTHDAY PARTY !

EVERYONE LOVED
THE LOCAL NEWSPAPERS
40TH BIRTHDAY
PHOTOGRAPH OF THEIR
TOWN COUNCIL TREASURER,
GERALD POSTLETHWAITE,
AS A NUDE 4 YEAR OLD
SITTING ON HIS POTTY!

SECRETLY, GERALD
WONDERED IF HE
SHOULD SHOOT
OR POISON
HIS MOTHER!

HA, HA, HA!
HE, HE, HE!
HA, HA, HA!

WHEN PHIL REGAINED CONSCIOUSNESS HE WOULD LEARN WHY IT HAD NOT
BEEN A GOOD IDEA TO BUY JILL THE 'FACELIFT AND LIPOSUCTION TREATMENT
PACKAGE' AT THE COSMETIC SURGERY CLINIC FOR HER 40TH BIRTHDAY!

ON HIS 40TH BIRTHDAY ERIC WENT BACK TO VISIT THE LITTLE MEADOW WHERE LAY THE OLD 'LIGHTENING TREE' THAT HE HAD PLAYED ON AS A BOY. UNFORTUNATELY THIS WAS NOT ERIC'S LUCKY DAY!

SOME POSITIVE 'FUN' THINGS TO DO TO OVERCOME THE FEAR OF BEING 40!

IF POSSIBLE THESE SHOULD BE DONE THE DAY **BEFORE** YOUR BIRTHDAY, WHILE YOU ARE STILL SANE ENOUGH TO THINK STRAIGHT!

FOR EXAMPLE:

JIM DECIDED TO CURE HIS SINUSITIS BY DRILLING OUT HIS NASAL CAVITIES WITH HIS POWER DRILL!

HELEN DECIDED
IT WAS TIME TO
FEEL GOOD ABOUT
HERSELF, SO SHE
TURNED THE
MAGNIFYING SIDE
OF HER MAKE-UP
MIRROR TO
THE WALL !

CAROL SHOWED TOTAL DISREGARD FOR HER
40TH BIRTHDAY BY BUNGEEY-JUMPING INTO A LIVE VOLCANO!

MARK DECIDED THAT DRIVING TO THE SOUTH OF FRANCE
WOULD BE A GOOD WAY TO TAKE HIS MIND OFF HIS 40TH BIRTHDAY!

EVERYONE SOON FORGOT ABOUT LINDA'S 40TH BIRTHDAY WHEN THEY SAW HOW WELL SHE COULD TIGHT-ROPE WALK IN THE NUDE!

JOHN SOON FORGOT ABOUT BEING 40 BY TAKING AN EXCITING TRIP TO A DISTANT PLACE WHERE NO ONE CARED HOW OLD HE WAS!

40 LOVE AND SEX FOR TEA

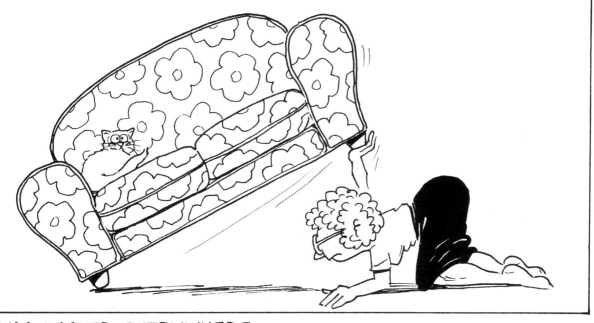

PYHLISS LOOKED EVERYWHERE
BUT SHE STILL COULDN'T FIND HER 'G' SPOT !

BELINDA DECIDED THAT SHE WOULD SPICE UP THEIR SEX LIFE
BUT MORRIS WAS TOO SCARED TO COME OUT FROM UNDER THE BED!

DICK WAS 40 AND FEELING FRUSTRATED, SO HE WENT OUT TO BUY A MAGAZINE...

HE BOUGHT A COPY OF PRACTICAL GARDENING!

AS THE BED MOVED ACROSS THE ROOM MAVIS COULDN'T HELP WONDERING IF SHE SHOULD DEFROST THE TURKEY OR THE VEGETARIAN LASAGNE FOR DINNER TOMORROW!

WHEN ROY ASKED BETTY TO GET A COPY OF 'THE PERFUMED GARDEN'
LITTLE DID SHE REALISE THAT IT HAD NOTHING TO DO WITH GARDENING!

FRANK HAD BEEN TOO EMBARRASSED TO BUY A PACK OF CONDOMS, SO HE'D BOUGHT A PACK OF DENTAL GUM INSTEAD. RITA WAS NOT IMPRESSED!

MICK AND JEAN WERE RE-DISCOVERING THE JOY OF SEX.
BY 'POSITION 7' THEY DISCOVERED THAT THEY BOTH HAD SLIPPED DISCS!

WHEN THE GIRLS GAVE KAREN A CHROME-PLATED VIBRATOR FOR HER 40TH BIRTHDAY SHE THOUGHT IT WAS SOME KIND OF EXECUTIVE TOY. THEN SHE DISCOVERED ITS **REAL** FUNCTION... AN ELECTRIC ROLLING-PIN !

SOMETHING TOLD VICTOR THAT PAM DIDN'T WANT TO READ TONIGHT!

SINCE JOINING THE WOMEN'S ASSERTIVENESS GROUP FAY SEEMED
TO HAVE PROBLEMS DISTINGUISHING SEX FROM UN-ARMED COMBAT!

PAUL AND JUNE HAD BOUGHT A 'BETTER SEX' VIDEO, BUT BY THE TIME THE SEX THERAPIST HAD FINISHED TALKING THEY WERE BOTH FAST ASLEEP!

THAT FORTY FEELING

MATTHEW
TACTFULLY REFRAINED
FROM MENTIONING
THAT HIS DAD WAS NOT
ONLY **NOT** SCORING
ANY POINTS...
HE WAS ALSO
PLAYING 'MEGASONIC
UPSIDE DOWN <u>!</u>

SEE, I'M
GETTING
REALLY GOOD
AT THIS !

BEEP!
ZAP!
BEEP!

SYLVIA HAD BEEN DETERMINED THAT BEING 40 WOULD NOT STOP HER PROVING TO HER DAUGHTER THAT SHE COULD ROLLER-DISCO AS WELL AS ANY 18 YEAR OLD!

KEVIN TRIED HARD TO DISGUISE THE FACT THAT HE WAS GOING BALD, BUT NO ONE WAS FOOLED!

BRENDA HAD
SPENT MANY SLEEPLESS
NIGHTS WORRYING
ABOUT HER WRINKLES
THEN ONE DAY
SHE WOKE UP WITH
CROWS FEET AND
HAD SOMETHING ELSE
TO WORRY ABOUT !

CLIVE HAD ALWAYS
BEEN A FAN OF
HORROR FILMS, BUT
WHEN HE WOKE UP ON
HIS 40TH BIRTHDAY
HE SUDDENLY REALISED
THAT NOW HE WAS IN
THE TWILIGHT ZONE
FOR REAL !

WHEN ANDREW CAME HOME TO FIND HIS SON WATCHING A 'DIRTY' VIDEO OF
SEXY NUDE LADIES DOING SEXY RUDE THINGS HE WAS ABSOLUTELY FURIOUS!
WHY DIDN'T THEY HAVE VIDEOS LIKE THAT WHEN HE WAS A TEENAGER!

HARRY LIVED TO REGRET NOT HAVING A HAIR TRANSPLANT!

JENNY AND JOAN HAD BEEN IN THE SAME SIXTH-FORM, BUT, STRANGELY, ALTHOUGH JENNY WAS NOW 40 JOAN WAS ONLY 34! CASUALLY JENNY PASSED HER COPY OF THEIR SIXTH-FORM GROUP PHOTOGRAPH TO JOAN'S NEW BOY-FRIEND!

NOW HE WAS 40
GILBERT NOTICED
A STRANGE
PHENOMENON...
WHEN HE TOOK HIS
BELT OFF, HIS
TROUSERS DIDN'T
FALL DOWN !

TIME HAD JUST FLOWN SINCE DOROTHY WAS A 5 YEAR OLD. PLAYING IN THE MUD ON HER GRANDFATHER'S FARM—NOW SHE WAS A 40 YEAR OLD COVERED IN MUD IN A HEALTH FARM. DOROTHY WONDERED IF ALL THIS HAD SOME PROFOUND SPIRITUAL SIGNIFICANCE BUT MOSTLY SHE WONDERED IF THEY'D REMOVED ALL THE WORMS!

RAY HAD REALLY
BELIEVED 'YOU ARE ONLY
AS OLD AS THE WOMAN
YOU FEEL'...
THAT IS, UNTIL
SHE HAD TO HELP
HIM OFF THE DANCE
FLOOR AND CALL
THE PARAMEDICS!

WHEN VAL ASKED, "IF THE PIXELS TOOK SO MANY BITES WHAT WOULD THE ELVES EAT?" IT BECAME OBVIOUS TO EVERYONE ON THE COMPUTING COURSE THAT HER I.Q. WAS PROBABLY THE SAME AS HER AGE—ABOUT 40!

UNLIKE MANY MEN HIS AGE, RUPERT WAS FIT ENOUGH TO TOUCH THE FLOOR WITH THE PALMS OF HIS HANDS. UNFORTUNATELY HE WAS NOT FIT ENOUGH TO STRAIGHTEN UP AGAIN!

ROGER KNEW HE WAS OVER THE HILL, WHEN HE SUCKED HIS GUT IN...

...AND IT STILL HUNG OUT !

MAVIS JUST HAD TO FACE IT— SHE WAS NOW A 'GOLDEN OLDIE'...
ALL HER FAVOURITE ARTISTES WERE IN THE EASY LISTENING SECTION!

YOU KNOW YOU ARE PAST IT WHEN...

SOMEONE BUYS
YOU A T-SHIRT
FOR YOUR
40TH BIRTHDAY
AND YOU'RE NOT
SURE IF IT'S A
JOKE OR A
DEFINITION !

SAMANTHA KNEW THAT SHE WAS ON THE VERGE OF IMPENDING SENILITY WHEN SHE SAT UP TILL 2 IN THE MORNING AND **STILL** COULD NOT UNDERSTAND THE QUESTIONS IN HER 12 YEAR OLD SON'S MATH HOMEWORK !

AND FINALLY... WHEN EVERYONE HAS RE-ENFORCED THE AWFUL FACT OF BEING **40**, THERE IS ONLY ONE THING YOU CAN SAY...